# For the Future of Girls

# For the Future of Girls

Poems by

Lisa Grunberger

Book design by Mariana Felcman
Author photo by Robert G. Margolis
Front cover art: "Pomegrante" by Svetlana Melik-Nubarova


ISBN: 978-1-63980-396-5

Kelsay Books
502 South 1040 East, A-119
American Fork, Utah 84003
Kelsaybooks.com

*For my mother, Rachel Broda Grunberger,*
*my homeland*
*(August 17, 1925 – November 2, 1992)*

# Acknowledgments

I gratefully acknowledge the following presses for publishing my work, sometimes in earlier versions and with different titles:

Brittany Noakes Award: "Genesis: Beginning the In"

*Born Knowing* (Finishing Line Press): "After the Rain," "Born Knowing," "Misfortune," "Yellow," "Genesis: Beginning the In," "When Eve Leaves"

*Bridges: A Jewish Feminist Journal:* "Go Buy Yourself Something Nice"

*Crab Orchard Review:* "Chef Richard as Jesus," "Evidence of Doors"

*Dialogi:* "On the Bus," "Like Mr. Touch" (a Slovenian literary magazine; these poems translated by Kristina Kocan appear in both English and Slovenian)

*Hanging Loose Press:* "When I Was a Woman"

*I am dirty* (Moonstone Arts Center): "I am dirty," "Preservation," "Red. Autumn. Star.," "To My Unborn Child," "Voice"

*In Our Own Words: A Generation Defining Itself:* "Moonlighting as the Mona Lisa in the Joan of Arc Park"

*The Laurel Review:* "Neighbors"

*Long Story Short Poetry Project: Ekphrastic Poems:* "Until nothing is left"

*Mizmor L'David Anthology* (Poetica Press): "Born Knowing"

*Mom Egg Review:* "Arrival of the Stars"

*Philadelphia Stories:* "Like Mr. Touch," "Secrets"

*Welcome to the Resistance: Poetry as Protest* (Stockton University Press, 2020): "A Story of the Letter *J*"

# Contents

Part 3. A Story of the Letter *J*

Part 4. Human Race

# Part 1
# Genesis: Beginning the In

# Genesis: Beginning the In

*A dream uninterpreted is like a letter unopened.*
—The Talmud

Now I will relive my mother
backwards, read her life
from back to front
from the moment she breathed
her last breath in my arms
after I pressed her mottled feet
into my sleepy hands
to the moment she picked olives
in Israel, made her little brother
pee in his pants at the movies in Tel Aviv
because Katherine Hepburn was kissing Spencer Tracy.
She lifts me into her cradled arms
and kisses my newborn forehead
in the Miami hospital.
By the time I'm done
a new story will birth
between my legs, a new letter will be open.
My mother will be newborn by then,
a babe in Palestine to a cross-eyed German mother
who rode a bike around the streets of Tel-Aviv,
spent money on *bon-bons* when she should have
been buying potatoes and onions and eggs.
Her father, a Russian Jew, loved his first-born
Rachel deepest, she said to me once
in the den while she mended damaged sweaters,
her glasses dangling from a gold chain around her neck.
Even when she was doing nothing, she looked wise.
I will gather the letters and begin again,
rocking Rachel in my new mother arms,
remembering always how she smelled of the lilacs
that grew by the fence in the backyard,
all summer the scent in the kitchen
fills me now.

# I am dirty

I was born
in a dirty month,
under a dirty blue sky.
Mickey, alligators, leaping dolphins
nearby, all dirty.

My dirty childhood dog
pawed dirty steps on
my dirty soul.

We ate a dirty soup of
mushrooms, barley and beans
while we watched the stillness
of the dirty bay feed
into the dirty Atlantic.

We continued our dirty cross-pollination,
hide-and-seeking, ricocheting,
gliding dirty over each other—
the dog, the parrot, the two cats,
the Jack Dempsey in the long fish tank,

the 1897 German-Czech Oma,
the steady Viennese Father's clocks,
part hum, part dirty-tick, the Israeli Mother's
robust dirty-apple yell overflowing
with cumin and paprika.

The child's tightly held
number two pencil
grips on the dirty world,
the child is beginning to
think dirty thoughts—
Van Gogh's ear,

Beethoven's heart,
Flaubert's parrots,
cutting and pasting,
using the dirty dictionary.

# The House Did Not Speak

Music played every fifteen minutes
and pendulums hung promiscuously,
heavier than the apples on the trees, and acorns,
cats and mice wandered the rusting shed

that housed rakes and mowers, the neighbor's son's
old motorcycle, blood dried on the deflated tires.
There were snow-powdered almond cookies
in the shape of crescent moons,

and one-and-a-half survivors in no shape
but what flesh gives rise to every morning
when some still thank God for open holes
through which piss and shit and tears can flow.

There was a white and brown dog,
who was fluent in Yiddish, English, and German,
and half-fluent in Hebrew, depending on the time of day.
Inside the house there was no history

but only fractured *toledot,*
on an unsuspecting suburban street
that faced a dirty bay,
repeated like a winter sky.

# Born Knowing

My father fixes clocks in the basement,
my mother watches TV upstairs.
My Oma's door is always closed.
I imagine she sits on the mint green chair
knitting or reading Goethe. On Saturday
she watches Lawrence Welk.
I sit at the kitchen table doing homework—
Iroquois Indians, algebra, *Pride and Prejudice.*
I taste the frozen cups of Weight Watchers
Butter Pecan ice treat buried underneath
supermarket chicken breasts and blue ice packs.
It tastes synthetic, its icy granules refuse
to melt in my adolescent mouth.

Sometimes Daddy comes up
and cuts himself a piece of smelly cheese
or pulls out a bar of Cadbury Milk Chocolate
and breaks off a piece for me.
Mom comes down in her pink slippers then,
during a break for commercials. She chases
a cricket whose chirping makes her nervous,
like a ticking clock does or water dripping.
She cuts a grapefruit into eight wedges and
places it in a bowl atop a Bounty paper towel
with another towel in hand to collect the juice.
She goes upstairs.

Between 1 and 4 in the morning the house
holds my Oma's screams. I don't remember
asking my mother the *why* or *what* of these cries.
I was born knowing about Buchenwald,
my Opa Leo who died of tuberculosis in a labor camp.
I knew how on the illegal ship to Palestine
my beanpole Dad ate raw potatoes and onions like apples.

Every morning I come down the stairs to find Oma
dressed in stockings and shoes, a silk blouse and tweed skirt,
drinking *Café Schwartz*—black coffee, facing the sun,
looking out at the bay. Never once did I think to ask her of
what she dreamed. But sometimes, when I was very young,
I would go to her, sit at the edge of her bed that
smelled of over-ripe fruit, yarn and Nivea cream,
and press my small hand to her forehead,
wet with Hitler's sweat.

# Sextant

I was not a strong student of science.
But in seventh grade, I won the science award
for my project on the sextant. I was embarrassed
to say the word "sextant." It had the word "sex" in it.
So I whispered it every time I said it.

"Sextant," I whispered, "an instrument for determining
the angle between the horizon and the sun or the moon."
I memorized that from Webster's Dictionary.
Mommy held open the page and dictated it to me.
I wrote it with a black marker on the oaktag

under the real sextant Daddy brought up from the basement.
I realize now, 20 years after he's gone, he probably helped
the Romanian captain of the Noemi Julia find their way
through the Mediterranean Sea. When he was 19 years old
and left Berlin, left his parents, left his life

as an engineering student so he wouldn't be murdered.
I see him holding the sextant in his elegant hands,
explaining to me in his mild gentle way how it works:
*Leeza, you see here is the circle that is marked like a sundial.*
But I could barely follow his words.

Now, when I need him to explain to me
something in the world, to navigate a narrow space,
he is not here, and I do not know where that gold sextant is—
precise and balanced, dignified, centered and calm,
like my father, sitting at the table in the gym

with all the other student projects on snails and digestion
and robots. But it was my sextant that won the prize.
I do not remember the day. And when I ask my father
what it was like to survive when his father
died in a labor camp, when I ask my father

what it felt like to survive when his Aunt Sofie,
his father's sister, and her four children died,
when I ask my father, how did you find your way,
he didn't say anything. He might have mumbled
something about finding Mommy, 15,

on the shore by the Mediterranean Sea,
when he was looking for something to eat.
*I was hungry Leeza, very hungry. We only had*
*raw onions and raw potatoes on the boat for many months.*
*It's not good to talk of such things.*

Sextant, sextant, where is my father, where did you
take him, and my mother too, and Omama, all of them
gone too early? For I was just beginning to be me,
and then I had to become me without them,
my center, my family, my compass, my sun.

And I look up into the autumn sky,
his favorite season and mine,
while Mommy liked summer, and Omama—
well, she was by then beyond seasons,
surviving her survival, but that

is a different story entirely.
I want to find the place
death takes the no longer alive.
Where have you taken my parents?
Guide me there, navigate for me

this place of silence from
where no one seems to return.
Send me a sign.

# Omama's Hands

1.

She would swing me from a thick rope
looped through a tire that hung from
the birch tree in the backyard
until it became sick with chemicals.
For years, we'd stare at the phantom limb birch,
now a stump where hula hoops
and rotten apples ended up.

We watched planes descend to Kennedy airport, *dirty birds,*
she crowed, through the chocolate bubbles of her *kalte café.*

The mushrooms for the *Schwammerlsuppe*
sit in pearl pewter mounds on the kitchen table,
porcini, portabella, cremini, and simple button caps.
She plays with fungus when she isn't knitting
or rereading *The Magic Mountain.*

Her hands have touched Hitler
I thought once as she lay them
on the baby grand's keys and caressed
the keys like light against an ancient map.

She pauses and inhales,
her high-heeled stockinged foot
presses down on the *fortissimo* pedal
slowly *mit gefuhl,* then Wagner fills
the suburban bayside living room on
the South Shore of Long Island and
makes my father's antique clocks buzz,
pendulums dance. Birds scatter
in schools of fright.

Her blue eyes close
over half a century.

2.

When I played Beethoven
on the baby grand,
I didn't need a metronome.

She was time, my beat, her long white finger,
sticking up, chopped into the suburban air,
a warning, keeping me steady

longing for her to tell me what they ate
*over there*. Knife and fork in hand,
a mannequin, she cut her steak
mechanically, indifferent and vain.

She had perfect pitch. When we fought
I called her *hexe,* witch, the only German curse
word I knew. She took it like a boxer takes a punch,
all 82 years of her a stoic stick of willed silence.

She spit on mahjong and B'nai Brith brunches.
*Bourgeois* she said to me once while we were chopping
mushrooms. *Do you know what this means?*
*Do they teach you anything?*

There were no answers in her body. To this day,
I do not know what she lived for over here.

# Metronome

My mother was the minute hand my father the hour.
The time was on the way to work.
The steeple is a greenish gray stretching
into the sky like a wire.

The light was red then green then red then green and
I taught these colors to my daughter
who moments ago was hugging my calf
like it was a Torah scroll.

The clouds are shifty as a banker.
The stars move fast on their silent metronome.
Winter arrived early today.
Everyone tells stories about its arrival.

I have not forgotten you, I say loud  then soft,
then slow then fast. These are words  she knows.
She has heard my voice say them
over and over again to the moon.

My mother ticks it's late,
my father chimes it's early.
Tomorrow we will set a ladder against a
mountain in Philadelphia and climb.

Maybe on the way we will see
time and death. More likely
there will be cherry blossoms,
their breath seconds away from being born.

# Rockaway

No one will ever be
as interested in returning
to my childhood town
with its dirty bay water

and seedy bars, the sweet waffles,
and the broken curb where the accident
occurred in front of the dry cleaners,
now a McDonalds.

No one will hear
my mother's voice say *come*
*to a complete stop at the stop sign*
by Quay Court where Diane used to live

on a delicious dead-end street
where we played kickball until dusk,
our ragdoll babies in strollers on the curb.
No one will care about

my long cross-country runs
around the high school track
counting my breath,
willing arms at hips to swing

like Mr. Buckery taught me,
loose and relaxed.
No one will care
about the mimosa in the front yard.

When it shed its pink-feathered petals,
it filled Mom's maroon Honda
with a hat of petals she
swept with the snowbrush

used in winter to scrape
ice off the windshield so
I wouldn't be late for school.
No one will care

about the bagel shop where
Dad and I used to go on Sunday mornings
after she died and buy too many bagels,
too much cream cheese in flavors

like blueberry and horseradish because
we were hungry to taste something new.
No one will care,
neither lover nor daughter,

how these streets speak to me.
This is the church where I took the Eucharist,
that is where I stole the watermelon Jolly Rancher
candies, and there, under the boardwalk,

the first deep tongue kiss,
where he cupped my breast at fifteen,
his sandy palm cupped it with such gentleness
my knees did shake,

and his other hand stroked my summer hair
until we fell down upon each other.
No one will care
how originally naked we were,

how quiet when the waves
came into our ears at dawn.

# Go Buy Yourself Something Nice

A child in Berlin, he bathed with Marlene Dietrich's daughter.
Einstein played the violin for the boys at the prep school.
Einstein wore sneakers.

He worked downstairs at night with timepieces,
eye loupe in left eye, hands steady as a surgeon's.
A stack of *palatchinka*, a low buttery laugh, never raised his voice.

When in college I tell him I'm in love with a woman,
at first he says nothing. Then:
*The important thing is to be happy.*

Once on a drive to Lake George: *When you were a baby,*
*this was all green. How many malls*
*does this country need?*

On Sundays he is under a car, face streaked with grease.
Roasted cashews and a funny movie. Ice cream at Friendly's.
Once he raced me down the street to the beach.

When he dies, I live in the house for years,
dance to his Louis Armstrong eight-tracks.
*Play the boogie-woogie for me, Leeza.*

Years after, I find a hundred-dollar bill
in his leather money belt,
folded in crisp thirds.

# Secrets

1.

When my father was moving
from being to being nothing
I was about to go for a bike ride.

His right hand rose up
from under the blue blanket
as he patted the bed for me to sit.

I sat and stroked his face
so thin and unshaven it appeared
slender as the Flatiron building.

2.

In summer we could sit in the yard for hours
eating cherries, throwing the pits
the dog would chase.
*We're planting cherry trees,* he'd say.

In winter we raced through bowls of green
pistachios, seeing who could crack them faster.
We'd set aside the sealed ones, the ones
that stubbornly refused to be opened,
the ones with no crack.

Daddy said they have secrets
they can't bear to share with us yet.
He poured the uncracked nuts
into a ceramic bowl.

He never disturbed the bowl
but sometimes he would lift it
as though it were a seashell.
He would nod his head.
He was a quiet man.


3.


I listen to my father's slow breath,
place ice chips on his cracked lips.
I listen to the final rattle and remember
a baby's noise maker, Daddy's keys.


4.


Any stillness I possess belongs
to a yard
where another family lives
in the midst of cherry trees
they cannot see.

# Yellow

It is late December and I want
to remember my mother's recipe
for almond crescents. If I remembered
everything, I would know if my father
lived through *Kristallnacht,* wore
a Jewish star his mother sewed.

I would know the name of the store
where Oma bought the thread—or did
she pull it out from one of Opa's suits,
a yellow seam from the inner thigh?
I would know what my father saw moments before
he boarded the ship, full of rotten potatoes and onions,
that took him to the illegal shores of Palestine.

The lists, I would not remember:
cat food, toilet paper, AA batteries.
I would not remember when I was nine
at Jones Beach, the day I ran into
ten-foot waves, tossed and turned into stone.
I would not remember floating in the Dead Sea,
holding hands with the stranger boy

from the summer youth bus,
his hand soft and hot and muddy,
his lips salty from California.
My fifteen-year-old nails dig into
his sunburned back. He shows me
the scars later by the fig tree, his T-shirt
rolled up to his narrow, freckled shoulders.

Shipped between statue and shadow
my father bites into a rotten onion.
The soot of Berlin's synagogues clings to his shirt.

He smokes a cigarette with a Polish boy,
flicks the ashes into the Mediterranean,
into which my mother, fifteen runs,
her hair golden curls, the boy behind her

a soldier, always a soldier.

# Rumors, or Two Barefoot Girls

*for M*


our dogs were having a love affair—
        that was the rumor when they ran away
                on those dusky winter days

when the snow rose over our hips
        and we rolled down mountains
                our fathers had shoveled.

We lived across from each other
        on a dead-end street,
                your mutt Snowball loved to sniff

my mutt Tammy's ass.
        They galloped across to the beach
                around the corner from the dead end,

we would run barefoot in the snow,
        my mother's voice running after us
                *come back girls, put on shoes!*

But we didn't feel the cold on our feet—
        just as my daughter today peels off
                her down jacket, runs round

and round a winter playground, you call
        to tell me you have the cancer that
                killed your father Ritchie, and you want

me to meet you in the city, to choose
        a wig for when your hair falls out
                *because it will fall out, there is*

*no turning back,* you say.
    Your voice is the voice
        of my childhood, my mother

with her thick Israeli accent
    calling us back to my house
        where you loved to sit in the kitchen

playing Rummikub on Saturday mornings
    while I slept and slept through the morning cartoons,
        through your second cup of hot cocoa

my mother spiked with thick
    Turkish coffee and whipped cream
        she beat herself, turning the whisk

round and round against the bowl.
    It was the turning whisk that woke me
        and now your daughter will be bat mitzva,

we secular Jews you and me, Meryl,
    continuing something ancient and amorphous
        from when we were Hebrew school dropouts:

I asked my mother the *brocha* for shrimp
    and she said enough, *maspik,* and your mother
        pulled you out too, *for Rachel is a wise woman.*

What is this thing we pull along, this Jewish thing?
    It is something nameless as the God it comes from.
        And I love you so much, I want to run

back barefoot to meet you at the beach behind
    my house where our white and brown mutts frolicked
        by the bay moving to and from the shoreline,

flirting with each other and the water.
      I see us both, now, looking at our own hair
            growing under our arms, between our legs,

calling your older cousin Robin to explain
      to us a line in a Judy Blume novel—
        *what does it mean to "come"?*

Midnight giggling under our make-shift pink tent, a bowl
      of Orville Redenbacher's popcorn, a Barbie camper.
      I will meet you where we used to live,

when our dogs were having a love affair
      and ran away and we chased them barefoot in the snow.
      We always found them.

Our rescuing hearts beating fast,
      they always came home.
      We held their collars

and walked home slowly, you went one way,
      I went the other, the dogs looking back at each other
      moving in opposite directions.

We pulled our blinds up and down,
      down and up to say goodnight, good morning,
      in our Morse code grammar

until your father died, then your eyes
      disappeared and I wondered where you went.
      Here I am, here you are now—

still two barefoot girls
      running through snow.
      Time to buy a wig.

# Part 2
# When I Was a Woman

# Until nothing is left

but the sparkling ruby slippers
of the Good Witch of the East
and Dorothy's tornado dreams.

Until nothing is left
but the brain the size of a nut
and a heart the size of a fist
floating in thinning blood,
no flesh, no ribs.

Until nothing is left
but a ring that keeps slipping
off a double-jointed finger,
a nail you polish over
and over again.

Until nothing is left
but the absence of a voice never spoken
lurking behind ruby red and polished toes,
bearing the weight of a hundred houses,
the lives of all the children.

Until nothing is left
but shriveled feet,
wrapped and stuffed to order,
a shimmering tiara taking a walk
along an extended stage,
a showcase of packaged bones
behind a dome of glass.

Until nothing is left
but the echoes of whistles
training us to foam at the mouth
and fetch the desired bone.

Until nothing is left
but camouflaged flesh beaten
with stick and stone words and made
to disappear behind bruised blooms.

Until nothing is left
but an invisible war whose cruelties—
kowtowing flowers, stamped yellow grass,
bulldozed forests, ruby-toed women, hang
down heavy from the weight of nothing,
nothing, until

nothing is left but
the space between the legs
through which children come and go.

# Butterflies and Beauty

The Costa Rican butterfly lands on my left breast
and all the tourists at the Museum of Natural History
shoot digital pictures of the butterfly and my breast.
Moments later a damaged butterfly lands on my head.
*Don't move!* a stranger shouts and shoots,
blinding me with the flash. A woman bearing
butterfly information (with red lipstick on her front tooth)
says, *butterflies are the pandas of the insect world.*
*They are a beautiful insect and that's why we care about them.*

She seems perturbed by this, as she has only recently
moved from beautiful for her age to invisible for any age.
She has a flat chest and skinny legs, crow's feet that shine
with expensive cream. *I dare you to stick your hand into the*
*sugar water* my 13-year-old cousin taunts.
*Let's cover you with butterflies!*
I stick my hand into the sweet water
on which the butterflies feast. I want to attract beauty—
come land on me, beautiful insects!

Butterflies live for two weeks. We do not kill them
because they are beautiful. I am forty and still single.
You are so beautiful and skinny, my young cousin, Tal
tells me all day long. Her name means dew in Hebrew.
Her hormones rage. She cries all the time. I tell her,
*do not marry the first man with whom you fall in love.*
*Why not?* she asks. She is sad because
no butterflies have landed upon her.

# Moonlighting as Mona Lisa
# at the Joan of Arc Park

My agent moonlights as a poet and a baker.
We sat and smoked one cigarette at the statue of Joan of Arc
on 93<sup>rd</sup> street at Riverside Park until the key arrived
like a miracle, an answer and an interruption.

That night I returned and told Joan
how my engagement broke like an old piece
of china in a sink of warm water.
I told her how my hands were full of minor cuts.
I told her about turning forty and wanting a baby,
she who had died at twenty sat high on her bronze horse.
I couldn't tell if she paid attention or was humoring me,
she who had jumped from the prison tower,
she who had died a virgin.

I smashed a bottle of wine upon her body, then
watched the blood drip down the horse's flank
into the cobblestones. Asked if she knew she was in
God's grace, she said: "If I am not, may God put me there,
and if I am, may God keep me so."

Each morning I sit at her feet and I try to be brave.
Each morning flesh burns outside my door,
horses stampede, subways roar.
I do not set flowers at her feet.
I climb on top of her, ride her until it's time to get off.

# She Gives Thanks to Children in the Park

Thank apples for snakes,
thank snakes for knowledge.

Thank mirror for distortion,
thank frame for preservation.

I thought I would keep you,
but you fell apart, flew away.

I will not bind myself to joy
but to Isaac's laughter,
his swinging legs clasped
around the branch of his favorite tree.

I will not blind myself
to the flying kisses he casts,
into the dark future of a girl

standing by a tunnel,
tattooed with graffiti they cannot yet read,
the tunnel where the moonlight hides
in shame for each letter's ink is still wet.

I will not wait for the angel either,
but grow my own wings,
stutter away into the appled sun.

# Eve Writ's Travels

Eve Writ moves across the mountain page,
her cheeks puffy with the dust of Sinai,
Egypt's mortar buried under her ragged nails.

The light is similar to the dark, its texture of moon,
sandpaper and snakeskin. Eve Writ moves slowly
from Jerusalem to Babylon, Persia, Spain, out of Egypt,

she misses a train again. Eve Writ does not stop
to taste the mirage. Eve Writ jumps rope, a coarse braid
made of horsehair and rooster's breath.

She kisses Liberty's chapped lips,
her torch circled by movie projectors and hairspray,
she pushes carts filled with potatoes and onions,

overhears talk of Vegas showgirls, she pushes
brushes and cigarettes, milk bottles and knives.
Eve Writ walks the cobbled streets of the Lower East Side,

longs for a child, many children, shelter,
something unbroken. Eve Writ gets a nosebleed
climbing a spiral staircase, a neck ache straining to see

the skyscrapers, she looks where language
melts into an open scream of *no* and *why,*
she buys earplugs, goes to the matinee

where she sits and allows herself a good cry.
Eve Writ sells the movie to strangers
after a long and bumpy flight to California

with a man she calls Buddy.
Buddy smokes cigars and golfs,
buys Ralph Lauren ties while Eve Writ

gives birth, shops. He likes to pinch
her ass when she peels stamps off envelopes.
She has a hospital named after Bud when he dies.

Eve Writ, in exile from her own disaster,
changes her name, crosses borders,
crumbs of starlight in her eyes,

death a dreidel around which children
gather and gamble, shouting out Hebrew letters
like snake eyes, old gypsy names, a toothache.

Neither young nor old, Eve Writ waits
to womb the world. In between her ears
books are always burning.

# When I Was a Woman

*Bloom undergoes many metamorphoses in Mabbot Street and
perhaps the least spectacular of these is his change of sex.*
—Anthony Burgess on *Ulysses*

the branches bowed to me, the bus's wet roar made my ocean eyes
tear, when I was a woman all knowledge was a bread of thorns, my
bird breasts raged for more. I was biblical, fallen, a drip with seed.
Flowers bloomed when I breathed. I slipped into indecency, was
arrested for impersonating an Italian heiress paralyzed from the neck
down. When I was a woman I built a room of my own, no wallpaper,
no yellow, brick by brick with a fire place that worked, when I was
a woman I slept alone and wept for more alone, I walked city streets
buying time with broken meters. When I was a woman I forgot
nothing. Confucius, Roosevelt, Mussolini, Walt Disney were my
children: bad, selfish, lost, evil boy-men. I was always hungry,
stared at marble statues for hours. I loved chicken wings and
pistachio ice-cream chilled champagne and black berries. I liked to
read Neruda naked on a mountain top in California where I could
smell the ocean's salt rise up, an offering just for me. This pleased
me, Lord, it did, when I was a woman the slender tires of 10-speed
racing bikes aroused in me elegance and symmetry, old horses
trotting down Old City Philadelphia on Continental Square carrying
Alabama tourists turned me into one myself, my mane blowing in
the June wind, the gold specks in my gentle eyes bulbous twilights,
darkness reconsidered for pitch. When I was a woman I liked the
small-boned feet of princesses, the muscled hands of kings. One
minute the sun, the next, a door opens—the future pours in.

# A Misfortune

*There are a great many opinions in the world, and a good half of them
are held by people who have never been in trouble!*
          —Chekhov, *A Misfortune*


We were at war but all I remember are his mushroom lips my back
pressed against the brick wall. It was cold, freezing cold, he thought
my sheep skin coat pretty, rubbed it with the back of his hand the
rims of our hats kissed and young girls walked by—*I'll show them
how it's done,* I thought, his tongue pressed into me. Later, he sent
me the Chekhov story *A Misfortune* and asked me what I thought it
was all about, *mechanically, breathless, driven, master, force,* each
word placed just so on the mantle, beside the antique clock and the
leather-bound Bible.

When you begin to swear things off they come in droves to your
door too late to hold one hand up in protest, as the other beckons to
come forth, too late for the yes and no charade. To learn what you
can live without to master this, drive it into you, swallow it, let it
sink ocean deep, then fearless go, breathless go, improper go,
devoted go, mad go, witch go, alone go, reckless go, mournful go.
Did I say we were at war, a whole world crumbling and I
felt nothing but this pull as if necessity itself had come to my door
and with a naïve swoon I surrendered to one thing when all along
it was another and another and another, one more, one more, one
more, deeper go, devoted go, unmoored go, the motion itself the
thing unseen.

# When Eve Leaves

*Expectations*

She thinks, when I fly away
it will be in a V-shape.
It will be elegant, formal—
two birds on a clothesline.
That night she headed south
along the shores of his caring
body. As though
she found
life in the veins
of a leaf.

*Rejoinder*

She is drunk on time passing,
the plump nature of plums.
Peonies on a windowsill in March.
Streetlights that pop at dusk.
Bicycles flying in mid-air off city curbs.
Red ceramic teapots.
Chrysanthemums—both the word and the thing. Hats
and scarves and gloves and socks.
The way, when love leaves, the heart aches
for that which can't be seen.
To think about umbrellas is to think about the world.

*Dinosaur*

You left
a footprint

of cement
near my lung,
close to
where Eve
is said
to have come out.

# Angel, Fork

I'd just moved in. Where are the forks?
I longed to be still after years of motion.
To put up my feet, but yours beat me to it, heavy as
a dead animal in my lap.

Chrysanthemums along the path,
a man with red and blue suspenders, chalk-white
hair, swings a golf club on a makeshift course.

Again the sun is setting.
I'm far away from the sea.

Belief: all day I chew on the word.
By dusk, I know. Like a bite down
on aluminum with teeth of steel,
a habit, like chewing tobacco.
I spit black liquid.

In a certain light, from a certain angle,
I could be mistaken for an angel
shedding tears of bile.

# Like Mr. Touch

He looks like Mr. Touch,
he who walked around my hometown
laying hands on things—fire hydrants,
grocery carts, trees, cars.

Once he touched me,
came up behind me,
pressed his hands lightly upon my back.
I turned to see his bearded face, blue eyes,

his mouth full of cement,
a hole of memory.
He walked away, a ghost.
He touched things

to make sure they weren't bombs.
In Hebrew the word for bomb
is the same as the word for pomegrante:
*rimmon.* A burst of red.

He had been to Vietnam.
No one knows he touched me,
bidding me to explode into a thousand seeds.
So he could rest.

# Chef Richard as Jesus

A friend sends me news. Someone we both knew has died. An old cranky cook with yellow teeth and shriveled balls he once tried to show me in the walk-in cooler where he aged the meat and kept the lobster tails frozen stiff. He is survived by two daughters and a wife who tried to ex him out but he resisted each time and was proud of that too he told me once on a winter afternoon.

I was laying out the silverware and he sitting at an unkempt table seemed to be speaking casually, polishing knives himself but he was hawk-like with huge hands and their proud liver spots, the scent on him of fish, veal stock and blood. He said in a low, almost sexy bedroom voice, the voice of a train about to go off its tracks, he said *I was a kid when I got married the first time and she had big tits I loved to rub myself inside them. My daughter from that union is pushing forty now and more like me than her mother, she has the gift to cook and stand for hours and the gift to lead like you.*

For this I was supposed to swoon in the empty shady room. I was to go and sit down with him, bring him a thick shot of espresso the way he liked it (and he made sure we all knew from Maria the salad lady, a short stout woman who chopped the salads tight and small, to Carlos the broiler man) we all knew Richard liked his coffee short and sweet, three sugars and with a shot of whiskey, but I didn't bring him coffee or sit with him that day I stood at his feet and we looked at the dining room, the white tablecloths delivered minutes before in plastic bags from the dry cleaners, the shiny silverware, the water goblets, the salt and pepper shakers and the bright sun coming through the curtains white and yellow reflecting the snow that had fallen the day before.

We could hear the sound of Jimmy, the owner, shoveling snow. He liked to do things himself, Jimmy, liked to be outdoors taking care of things.

Chef looked at me and said, low and clear, *You don't really belong here ,do you? Where do you think you belong? Your father died last year, right? What was his name? I want to know his name. Do you look like him? My little one, unfortunately, she looks like me and her mother.*

Not a beauty, the second spouse of the aging chef. *She knows how to spend money like it's going out of style. I'll probably die in that kitchen. How did your 'ol Dad die, do you want to tell me anything about yourself? It's February and I'm tired and old and I like to watch you move across the room. You move like a gazelle, a tall Jewish gazelle. I usually don't like Jewish women but you, you're different, you listen to what I'm saying, don't you?* And then he beckoned me with a thick index finger to come over and showed me a postcard he made into business cards: Da Vinci's painting *The Last Supper* with himself as Jesus in the center.

He threw a knife at me once and called me a cunt and tried to reach under my skirt while I was digging for some cheesecake in the freezer. He said heaven would be filled with Swedish bombshells and he said he fucked an amputee and he said concentrate, make sure the plates are clean, and he said *Hitler didn't kill the Jews, I'll kill them with the lobster pie, it's got a stick of butter and a cup of cream,* and he said *Wanna see my new car? I have a vanity plate that says "Alterkocker."* And for years he said *I'll die here behind the stove stirring this fucking pot,*

but he didn't. He died in a room he never lived in and he was eighty and grumpy, still hungry for more cutting more garlic more tomatoes more stock more cheese more wine more words and women, more story, more whiskey, and yes more whiskey, swimming invisible in the black coffee.

# On the Bus

The stranger touched me
as though I were
a piece of sculpture,
the bus a museum,
the driver the guard.
The stranger was nine.

He chewed a strand
of black licorice
like a sailor,
touched my hip
as though he wanted
to dance.

He was alone
in the city
raining monkeys and stars.
He carried a bag of books.
Placed a book on my lap.
Piled them up.

Nabokov, Shakespeare,
*Mad* magazine, Sylvia Plath.
*Do you have children?* he asked,
tapping his finger against the glass—
a boy-man on a bus
at 8 a.m. heading to third grade.

The driver winked at us,
opened the huge door
and he spilled out.
I felt my frame sweat,
longed for a cigarette.

# Preservation

*The Pen*

On the night I betrayed you
my writer's block ended.
My pen wouldn't stay still,
moved across the page
intense as a monkey's play.

I heard garbage cans overthrown.
wanted the wind to make me want
your arms. But it didn't.
It made me want nothing
but the wind and my pen making love again.


*Dirty Girl*

Throws grapes into my mouth.
            *Take off your blouse.*
Wine from his open palm pours
upon my breasts, leg up on his chair
breadcrumbs on my knees.

He never touched me, love.
But I swallowed his smoke.
It's inside my lungs,
coating delicate tissues
no one can see.

*The Mannequin*

On the night I betrayed you
the wind sounded like an ambulance
come to extinguish me.

In your absence, I see
with mannequin hands.


*Envoi: The Silence*

There is a spring silence when the tulips tango.
A summer silence of low tide watermelon buzz.
A fall silence of roadside pumpkins.
A winter silence of discarded Christmas trees,
like corpses lying on curb sides.

The silence of wedding vows,
pink-frosted and too sweet.
The silence of politicians
cutting into their filet mignons at three.

The salty, sinking silence of ink.
The silence of a rock on a gravestone.
The silence, twisted and beauteous, is
a DNA double-helix ornament.

If you stir silence it turns
to mud or lace or grass,
depending on the time
of day and the color of your eyes.

# Ant-Whale

I woke up swatting the silence.
The silence moved, mountainous and quick.
The shadow cast by the bed, an elephant.
Swatting silence, like fanning the dead, I thought.
I stood on the bed, palmed the ceiling,
made a smacking noise, shook the bed.

I thought, this is the opposite of sex,
this swatting silence like a fly.
Swatting, like this, is a small death.
I stood on the bed corrected.
Where is the whale, I cried.
I wanted to stick my head into something big.

An oven, a dragon, a window would do.
I wanted to be devoured, eaten up.
I grabbed handfuls of air, mouthfuls of space,
became drunk on emptiness.
This went on for a long time.
The sun rose.

Naked, I went outside,
stuck my tongue out at the sun,
stuck my hand through people's bodies.
I smacked and swatted my way through streets,
as though my arms were knives,
wild clearing a wilderness path.

A kiss is like an ant and a whale.
An ant-whale. With this I was saved,
although I wasn't kissed for days.
One night I swatted my own reflection.
Pushed self-shards into the toilet's rusty mouth.
I swam through rooms of emptiness,

breast-stroked stair-bones, eyelids, armpits.
People stared.
I didn't wash my hair.

Then I became the space itself.
A fly on the wall.
Invisible until hunted.

# Park Avenue Abortion

I imagined
a clean, well-lit place
where the receptionist
is paid enough to smile,
where there are beautiful
people waiting in beautiful
rooms to mitigate against
the unbeautiful immanent thing
that always seems
to happen elsewhere.
New York City is where
I was supposed to have
my Park Avenue abortion.

But it didn't quite work out that way.
Teddy—that was his name,
had slipped a drug into my drink,
and the next thing I know
I wake up alone
in his Hell's Kitchen
apartment. I go home,
alone in my black party
dress on the LIRR,
to the house where
I grew up, filled with
nothing but dust and the baby
grand piano beside
my father's grandfather
clock. Everyone had
died, you see, and left
me with everything
and nothing. I was
looking for a husband,

only 29, orphaned
and in grief. Teddy
seemed promising
on the phone,
and in person
he cut a nice figure.
More than good enough.

And there I am lying on a table,
five weeks later,
legs splayed open in stirrups
drugged by a doctor
on a Park Avenue
that was not Park Avenue
(I wasn't thinking
straight)—a Park Avenue
in Long Island not Manhattan,
the third dark floor inside a strip mall.
I leave the clinic scraped clean.

After the mistaken
Park Avenue abortion
I met no less than
three other women
who all looked like me,
and who all said
I looked like them,
at a mixer
on the Upper West
Side. We gasped
when we learned
that two of us had
gotten pregnant by Teddy,

all of us victims
of his—what is it called,
when you drug a woman
and fuck her and come inside
her and then leave her lying
there asleep? Where did he go?
To visit his mother? Was it part
of his sick ritual? You see, he
mentioned her to all four of us.

This all happened over
twenty years ago, and now
that I'm a mother of a daughter
who asks me about blood
and pimples and boys,
men like Teddy return to me.

There were others
who tried to fuck me,
others who did not care
about consent, others
who I gave consent to
but who didn't care
about my pleasure
and those in the middle
who cared, but not enough,
who cared, but couldn't get it up
or who would not go down,
others who cared too much.
Needy men, soft men, hard men,
anxious, tired, scared, groping,
loud, boring men.

You have to care
about your own pleasure
I don't tell my daughter yet.
You have to be vigilant
and guarded and carry mace
I don't tell my daughter yet.
You have to study hard
I hear myself saying
and build something of your own.
Let the boys come to you.
Who is it that is saying this?

In this chapter,
of grief and vodka,
when my world fell apart
(this chapter that eventually comes to us
all if we're not playing it too safe),
the chapter where I try to find
my moorings after great loss,
consecutive loss after loss:
mother, father, grandmother, aunt,
dog, uncle, mother's car, father's car,
in this chapter, I had to rename
the world and begin again.
There's no getting around that part.

I wonder if I'll ever tell her
about the Park Avenue abortion.
I wonder what she will do
given the war on girls,
given men like Teddy
who golf with senators.

He kept calling me,
harassing me for months
like he did with the others.

I don't remember being knocked
out, don't remember him entering
me or exiting. The thing is, I lost time
that night. It's left a dark blank
spot in that day. When will it end,
to make a girl, a woman, give life
that comes from violence?
The assault is too much to bear.

To have had to give birth
to something of this monster,
to have to remember it
every day, its blank origin
made out of violent violation.
It sickens.

What to tell my daughter
about blood and boys
and hands and sex and the long
innocent sleep in his bed
until I wake up without blood,
filled with a beginning
I cannot begin. I could barely
feed myself in those days
without my loved ones
to protect me. It takes
time to build a life.
It takes time to become a human being.
It doesn't happen overnight.

That's what I will say to her.
It takes time to become a *mensch.*
I'll use one of my mother's words,
and that might make it easier,
to borrow wisdom from my dead.

# After the rain

the puddles in the lawn chairs reflect trees,
lost leaves like a man with a receding hairline.
After the rain the ache of fall settles in the air
like spider webs atop the bushes.
Worms invade my dried Turkish apricots
and the chicken is under salted. After the rain I crave
oatmeal walnut cookies and a glass of milk,
I crave sex, hard and raw, to stop time yes,
hard sex that stops time, something to chew on,
like taffy, raw beef, seaweed mineral rich.
After the rain I run five miles leaping over puddles
Kierkegaard-style. I listen to Coltrane and Neil Young,
Elvis Costello and Janis Joplin, I break open
the red when sufficient time has passed between
the fall of the sun and the rise of the moon,
after the rain I want the carnival to come to town
to set up a tent between the church and the abortion clinic
and I want all the kids with A. D. D. to throw away their drugs
and all the tired mothers to get drunk and I want to sway
my hips until the birds start singing their song and
I want to know a man who understands the Saturnian rings I make,
the circular twists and turns of my body's often sloppy penmanship
I want him to know how I dot my i's and cross my t's
I want him to dot my i's and cross my t's
O Lord, after the rain I'm so wet I don't know what to do
with the only body I've been given and given and given.

# Part 3
# A Story of the Letter $J$

# A story of the Letter *J*

*I had to stop here and there in order by resting to allow
my Jewishness to collect itself.*
—Franz Kafka, *Diaries,* November 1, 1911

A *J* spray-painted on my olive green house in South Philly,
its white-hooked tail grazes my daughter's head.

*A skinhead,* says my neighbor Jorge,
*un racista blanco, no entiendo,*

holding my hand inside his hand
far longer than any gringo would.

He smells of sawdust and cologne.
I shoot a picture with my phone

of my daughter underneath the *J*.
Evidence is always good to gather.

She traces the letter with her small finger.
She's just learning about how letters

make words and words make sentences.
Doesn't yet know sentences can kill:

*Arbeit macht frei.* Sentences can lie:
*Make America Great Again.* Sentences

can heal: *I have a dream.* She's fished
a pen from my bag and draws a *K* beside the *J*.

A new story begins. Across the street
Mozart seeps out of the second story.

Twelve-year-old Anita from China,
Jorge and I look up, as if music

were something to be seen, as though
it were something we could hold onto.

*I'll paint for you,* he says solemnly.
*It will be like new, like it never happened.*

# Not a memory

It is not
a memory
or shadow

not my mother's
or my father's
silence

it is the smell
of rotten onions on a boat
called the Noemi Julia

it is the dead apple tree
in my back yard
chasing him chasing me

around and around
the sea smell of the Mediterranean
in Long Island

it is not a word
but is composed of letters

it is not a riddle
there are no hints
it is not solvable

or treatable
it is inherited
or not

felt or forgotten
or not

it is not a job
for a detective
or a mourner or a mother

it begins and ends the same way

with fear, a hand raised,
one person, many people,
a podium, blood, uniforms,

not knowing themselves,
people without
faces

standing in the rain
hating the rain
hating the space
between their teeth

# Genius

Some genius, some Einstein,
needs to come out into the rain,
look rain in the eye
and design a new umbrella.

For today, sitting in this cafe
I saw a thousand umbrellas
rise and fall as though they
were kites or birds or children.

I saw adults wrestle with dying
windswept umbrellas and children cry
because of this billowing brokenness.
And old women I saw with canes and bags.

And I saw their struggle
against umbrella until they fold,
surrender to awning for shelter,
until they surrender to the rain itself.

Some genius, yes, needs to create
a new canopy for us.
For we seek
a different kind of shelter.

# Red. Autumn. Star.

The red bird
often mistaken for one
was not a macaw
it sang not me not me
in winter and in spring it sang
not yet not yet.

The man was not dead.
Often mistaken for that
he said not yet not yet
in autumn and in summer he cried
not that not that.

The house was not a home.
Often mistaken for one
its curtains crowed cold it's cold
in winter and in spring,
close the door close the door.

The stars were dead a long time.
Often mistaken for light
they twinkled we're drunk we're drunk
in summer and in fall look up look up
we're so beautiful you'll forget.

The prisoners were tired.
It was rumored there were miles
to go before they arrived.
Winter lingered like a red bird.

Close the door we're drunk
look up you'll forget
It's so early so early
you haven't been born
Not yet not yet.

# Witness

I dreamt of God in the witness chair,
fidgeting on the pale wood,
fingers busy counting stars.

Twelve Richard Geres sat on the jury,
their Zen-calm hands in orange-robed laps.
Gere's gaze was steady as a drunken goat.

When the feminists stormed the court,
the judge was naked, all hell broke loose.
The lawyers scratched their porcupine heads.

Then the black letters
danced around God,
who was filing Her nails.

My mother came with an apple cake
on a grand platter with a doily and a pot
of tea, across a moat filled with bullets.

Mom, when did this happen? When did you
become a traitor? Did you really love me? I
felt so loved, so secure, so needed.

I was crawling through mud,
slinking through a foreign field.
I saw a child dig a grave for her mother.

I pointed the cake at the witness.
When the Rebbe of Prague
arrived in a chariot, I didn't know

if it was meant to be funny or sad, but
I would have done it all over again.
God bowed deeply and my mother

wiped the mud off my naked body,
and gathered the spilled bullets
with her open mouth like a dog.

# Imagined in the 21<sup>st</sup> Century
# East of the Mississippi

To be an Eastern European poet circa 1950—
too many people stuffed inside small spaces and you,
writing quantum poems on large canvases.

*Do not use the words,* Grandmother says.

*Do not play the broken violin,* Uncle groans,
his forehead a map of places that no longer exist.

Do not watch the sculptured flags sway
in the grey wind or dream about time
          in a camp.

        Your attraction to him
when you were both young—
those thick Jewish lips
        trembling in the snow—

you should have kissed him then
when language was still half-alive
when you could still smell the urge to pray,

A knock on a door echoes.
You say I was a poet then.

# The Deceased on Leave

*for Jan T. Gross*

Really, you could leave me your boots,
missy. But Mrs. Joseph, I am still alive.

Well, I wasn't saying anything,
only that those are nice boots.

She comes over the next day.
Tells me, it's the end, missy.

She looks at my feet.
She had been a good neighbor.

She felt my boots were her boots
now that I was among the living dead.

The deceased on leave,
one historian calls us now.

I gave her the boots right before
I was deported.

I am dead,
speaking to you,

telling you to repeat
this tale

between two neighbors
in Poland, two mothers

who nursed our babies
together.

Hear her footsteps
in my kitchen,

walking on the streets,
shopping for pears and meat

in my boots.
She could smell

my body burn.
The boots

were too small,
her feet, squeezed

into that
small space,

hurt her
as she walked.

She slept
and rested her feet

in my bed.
This too is

what happened.
Repeat this

wherever you go
whatever you do.

# Villanelle: Repair

The repairs took longer than they'd hoped.
The kind neighbors brought wood for the fire.
They sat around the burning wood telling jokes.

The roof was leaky, the laundry got soaked.
Late into the night, someone called someone a liar.
The repairs took longer than they'd hoped.

Someone in town called them simple folk.
The young girl at the market felt someone sneer.
At night, they sat around the burning wood telling jokes.

When the father laughed, it was like a clock's stroke
but still there were nights and days filled with fear.
The repairs took longer than they'd hoped.

The tick tock of the antique clocks were strikes
of time, of music, a kind of lyre.
They sat around the fire telling jokes.

When the time of lilacs came near
they knew it would soon be over.
The repairs took longer than they'd hoped.
They sat around the burning telling jokes.

# Arbeit Macht Frei: In Three Parts

1.

Like fumbling street magicians,
the five thieves stole the sign.
It wouldn't fit into the car.
They sawed it into three pieces.

The winter branches, heavy with crystals,
can't help their piccolo siren.
I am free from eyes and memory.

A freshly pressed shirt, a silver letter opener,
a pair of brown socks, letters from his wife and mistress,
a gold pocket watch in a secret compartment
where nylons and garters might be hidden,
my grandfather's suitcase sits among 3,800 suitcases,
2000 kilograms of human hair, shoes, spectacles.


2.

I do not want to dream triumphant dreams
of hope. Sentiment sticks to me like lice.
I shave my heart until it barely beats.

All is so expertly broken.
The clouds clown with each other,
strip for sun and moon.

People don't know how to put on wings.
I give them safety pins,
but it's no use.

3.

The forensics expert smiles for the Polish cameras.
The chairman of Yad Vashem calls the theft
"an attack on the memory of the Holocaust."
A new movie emerges from the rubbish.
The actor starves himself at a Swedish spa
to prepare for the part.

In the meantime, a duplicate sign, prepared
five years ago—when the original was
being refurbished, has been put up.

# The Evidence of Doors

begs for a footnote.

Hitler walked through doors
kissed no mezuzahs the record shows,
ate vegetables and fruit outdoors
on a long picnic table

that could have ended up a door
but was fated to be a long table
around which SS soldiers ate *wiener schnitzel*
chugged *Gewurztraminer,* bit into crisp apples.

The table could have been the door
the door could have been the tree
from where Hitler's apple fell.
He liked his apples tart.

Devoured sweets late into the night.
Other men smoked pipes.
When Eva Braun walked through the door
heads like trees to spring turned.

Leni Riefenstahl put down her camera
to stare at Eva's body
the way a new prisoner stares at his cell door,
the way a watchmaker stares into the gears of a watch.

Maybe doors serve no evidence at all.
Maybe doors shoot blanks.
Hitler never entered Eva.
Eva entered Hitler a thousand times.

Stars flickered. Fruit fell off trees.
Polish sausage ate the sunlight.
Hitler loved how Leni could shoot naked bodies.
Did Hitler come yet?

Smoke spirals up
steeple-like into your open mouth,
a door. It's raining Hitler.
He's fetching his paintbrush.

# Angels Steal My Best Lines

Lying in my summer bed
watching the sky, mottled

as my mother's dying feet.
Phrases, maudlin memories

sometimes bubble up, like
I'm a thief with amnesia.

The angels steal my best lines.
By day's end, I'm left with nothing.

After midnight, the fun begins.
A flood of memories and no lifeboat.

I begin to clean the house:
a nameless toothbrush under

the sink with worn bristles,
my father's hat made of beaver fur.

When the angels come, I'm ready.
Sometimes, if they are in a good mood,

we play like carefree children
atop a steep silver slide.

Sometimes I still forget why I am here,
why I remain. Then the angels steal

this line too, and I clean and clean
until dawn breaks. I awake,

bruised with the color of work.
It is good, for remembering

is hard and it is always late.

# Part 4

# Human Race

# Zen (a poem)

I'll tell you this much—
this is what I know,
and still want to know:

I belong to my mother's
    last breath

    and my father's last kiss.

I belong to
    my Omama's
    nightmares,

    my Tante Geeska's
    always packed bag

that sits at the door
like an ancient watchdog,

a perpetually ripe
    banana on top,

a black and yellow comma.

I belong
to
        Time
and its
        opposite.

# To My Unborn Child

1.

I want you more than I wanted another kind of love.


2.

How Jerusalem has changed they say
when you have been absent for so long.

The bread has been sliced
with the silver knife you will inherit.

In the midst of war with bloody teeth
I wanted to cradle you.

People said, you are too old—

>    They nod knowing heads,
>    I point them to my mother's empty womb
>    of which I am the fruit.
>    I point them to the mercy of pomegranates,
>    Eliyahu's cup, my father's snores—

I am not old enough.

3.

My palm is already the shape of your skull.
Already the waves of your breath lull me awake,
you remain distant and foreign,
close and familiar, like the highest branch
on the mimosa tree near the rusting shed.

I have translated your cries into a thousand tongues.
I push the carriage up the hill,
Camus calls me back to the neon bar.

Before you, I worshipped idols,
after you, the mystery of summer snow arrives.


4.

I have no grandparents to spoil you,
no cousins to play with you,
no uncles to tease you, no aunts to
stuff crumpled dollar bills into your sticky palm.
I am sorry for this, my child.
But I have music and eggs and apples and light.
Come. We will bake my mother's apple cake.
Watch me slice the apples into quarter moons.
Pour them in. Be messy and wild.
I smell you near me, cinnamon and spice,
chosen as I was and am and you inside.
Come out to play in this open field
of momentary grace and stuttering fog.

# View

The man with the perpetual cart,
who never sells his paper bags,
stands beside a fire.

Jazz is too happy,
Jewish music too sad, Stalin said.
He banned both.

A woman pauses from buying chickens
and begins to dance. The Mexican boy

selling fish stops to look down at the birds.
The scent of fresh bread, fresh coffee,

the scent of homeless mixes with early winter, old grapes.
Cars drift like mounds of sand on a frozen beach.

You are as close as starlight,
as far as the mail dropped
moments ago into the box.

From the window she wonders
how the inside will come out,
the outside in.

# Arrival of the Stars

The stars arrive but they are too small.
And they need light to glow light.
A flashlight by the bedside is recommended.

We peel them off one by one.
It takes time. You stand on a desk,
I below you. We begin. I apply light

to a star and I hand it to you
barefoot on a desk made of walnut.
There is no darkness yet, and it cannot be rushed.

We wait until dusk arrives
to see our day's work.
Stars scatter the ceiling we have come

to call sky, then heaven, then gold buds,
an infant's lips. Soon she will

suckle my breast, a star of milk.
One day we will give each small star
a story, we will fatten them up,

give flesh to light, however small.
This is what we do, we wait for the stars
to arrive and we look.

# Momentary

Cherry blossoms arrive,
enter and exit on the narrow street.

Sometimes a single branch,
sometimes the tree itself.

The cuckoo today
keened in an elegiac tone.

It flew away
but its echo remains.

In the last ultrasound
you held the umbilicus
the way Lady Liberty
holds her torch, the way
a warrior holds a sword.

Will you be a tightrope walker,
my girl, with cherry blossom eyes?

Tell me you know
how to contort time.

Tell me this season
will be different.

# Voice

What will your voice
sound like

once it comes
out of your body

like a first rain first
    snow    first wind?

Hail, sun, bird, I've become an idolater,
    Lord,
        almost a murderer
        as I squeeze her in my midnight arms

how will I protect her
wrap her tease her

into this thing called
language,
                the cut of life

how will I unwound her
from
        the noise of redemption

so busy revealing itself
outside the window at the bus stop

in front of a pyramid of seedless grapes?

# Inheritance

That photo taken in still Mandate Palestine,
Mom around 19 with Tante Geeska
and Uncle Bela, near the piano bench,
plump Mom standing, her hair coiled,
a fitted caramel sweater up to her neck.
Matching skirt. A painting of trees above the piano.

Their expressions look as though they are all
responding to a different joke:
Geeska's wide smile, Bela's sad boyish face,
emergent jowls, and Mom with the Cheshire grin
of a new wife, always looking as though she knows
more than she will ever let on.

Bela's sturdy leather shoes,
Geeska's dainty doll-like in black ballet shoes.
She never reached more than four feet ten.
Mom's feet forever absent here,
what year is this—1944?
What happened to that picture of the trees?
What happened to the piano?

What happened to Bela's sadness?
In this 21$^{st}$ century room none of them
has ever seen I sit 70 years later,
my bare feet under an inherited table,
like two fish inside the Lusitania's window.

A toddler lives here too. She names
things and plays with the words.
In the bath, duck *rises to the surface*
becomes *Big Apple Circus.* I call her
by my mother's name. Today she pat
my head and said *good Momma,*
the three syllables an inheritance,
a lifetime of labor.

# Memories of Mother, Again

in the morning when my head is heavy with night and blanket
I am filled with you, your eyes in-between tiger and hazel dance

before me, and all day you will be there, a shard of the other
world inside me the way our house lives inside me

as real as a rain in a different country as real as a horse
from a different century, for we are still there aren't we, Mother,

turning over the Rummikub tiles, letting the Turkish coffee boil
again before pouring the dark thick brew into porcelain.

What does memory do if not bend around itself—it too
like a slant shadow broken on a summer street at noon.

Some see auras; my gifts are more modest: I smell your scent,
like a dog smells the roasted meat from a neighbor's feast under

a tent in the cul-de-sac around the bend where the houses
cost more because there is a garden and a view of flowers.

You always said follow the land and the water,
when we lay in bed watching and watching the boob tube,

that fluorescent wonder of sights and sounds,
your freshly set honey hair stiff to my touch when my face

would accidentally graze its edges. The early April land is full
of cherry blossoms. My daughter longs to meet you.

*What are you doing?* I ask when she places
her cool cheek against my heart? *Listening*

*to your mother's voice,* she says,
as though it were obvious.

# Neighbors

1.

My neighbors are always in shadow behind a screen,
seem to be fixing food, two thin ghosts moving
back and forth from stove to lamp passing each other without
saying a word. Sometimes the man steps out onto the stairs
with only his shorts on and he opens his skinny arms
in an expansive stretch. Then he refills the cat bowls with milk
from a half-gallon carton that seems too heavy for him to handle.
I hear the clang of my neighbors' silverware when they eat.
They usually eat eggs and toast. They drink a lot of coffee.
I smell it from across the narrow street. The woman,

who wears black leggings and a thin sleeveless blouse,
once burned the toast and I could smell that too. Just last week
at about midnight the sweet scent of maple syrup wafted
into our living room through the screen. They must be having
French toast, I said. Since then I've wanted some.
When the man is very hungry he scrapes the knife
on his plate and I feel it in my bones.
I've been wanting to bake a blueberry pie and bring them two
fat slices to see if they will let themselves smile. I've not seen
their faces but I imagine them drawn and long and sad.
Or maybe they've lost a child. Or one of them is sick.
I hear her clink-clinking her spoon on the rim of a glass.
Turning on the faucet. It is summer and I eavesdrop through
screens the way fruit-flies gather round over-ripe
peaches. Maybe I'm more lonely than they.

2.

I admire my neighbor watering her plants in front of her house on
this old South Philly block. Red flowers I cannot name sprout
from a yellow potholder. Inside my neighbor's house are books
and books on genocide. Sometimes a children's book springs
up between the books on death. Dr. Seuss keeps Stalin company.
It is like finding a green M&M inside a raw sirloin, blood pooling
into the mashed potatoes. It reminds me of my mother's bookshelf
where *Mein Kampf* stood beside *Robinson Crusoe* and *Jaws*.
The neighbor's body is voluptuous as a Dresden doll.
She sports a blonde bob and speaks German. Sometimes we
speak German together at her kitchen table over wine and cheese.

We have not known each other for a long time
but we've talked of sex, pregnancy and death.
We've fed each other's cats.
The intimacy of women is strange and immediate.
Once, she said and did not say *my great Uncle Max
was a Nazi,* and I said and did not say
*my Opa Leo died in Buchenwald.*

Then we filled each other's wine glasses
and drank in afternoon silence
until the children poured in, blonde and brown,
sticky with sweet mischief, curious, and hungry.

# Lying on the loft bed

my daughter and I
play with shadows,
our hands dance in space,

against the white walls,
become whales and crows,
and *Mommy put your finger*

*there, look, the fish is eating*
*my hand!* She holds the light
in her hand and commands

me not to move my fingers.
She moves the light round
and round tilting it to and fro

so the shadow of my hand
becomes large then small, bulbous black
tarantula turns slender octopus.

*Mommy, your knuckles look like a tushy!*
My still hand hovers in the air,
all around there is movement

and light and laughter and not yet
time to go to sleep, to close
our eyes and call it a day

I say *this is weird but*
*imagine my hand is God,*
and she says, *but you say*

*you're not sure God exists,*
and I say, *today, let us play*
*hand is God.*

She is game to play,
but skeptical still,
the shadows of my hand

moving across the ceiling and walls
are people (it sounds like Plato's Cave,
which I do not say)

and she says, *but your hand*
*can't be God, Mommy, it's just*
*your hand. Now you hold the light*

*and I'll hold my hand in the air*
*and you move the light around*
*and let's just be quiet*

*and watch my hand.*
*Can you see it? Mommy,*
*it's a dog with a hat—*
*what's that word for the side view?*

*A profile,* I offer. *Yes, a profile*
*of a girl eating a butterfly,*
*can you see it, Mommy?*

And then I say, *silhouette,*
and she is quiet
and repeats it, *silhouette—*

*it sounds like a soft song.*
We lie on her loft bed
past the time to sleep

and we whisper the word
*silhouette silhouette silhouette*
until our hands fall down

as if two stars disappeared
from a night sky
and we fall

into sleep
and it is good,
a dream of God

holding a light
moving us
towards and away

seek and hide
closer and farther
from the light

# Sometimes the way

the black cat leans against the windowsill
like a little drunk bald man with a loose tie around
his wrinkly neck, you think he is a cousin come alive
inside a different body, his purr in the morning light,
a pitch similar to this cousin's voice when he had
an extra cup of wine at the Seder.

By noon you know you're wrong and worry
about more important things, like misspent youth,
an old report card found inside a box covered
with cobwebs. It serves you right, for you spent
too much precious time thinking of the past,
dreaming of how memory is like, say, a pair of sunglasses

at some hotel you left to catch a plane, and once
on the plane, escaping a bad boyfriend, you can
see the glasses, their funky green frames, sitting
on the clean counter of the hotel desk where
they greet you with such wide smiles you think how
you could be happy, so happy. By dusk the cousin

returns, to join you for a glass of cabernet, the cat
climbs on your lap and begins to purr a purr you know
well, you take another sip and he is there with you,
this cousin, insisting on reading the fourth question

because he is not wise, because he is impatient
to eat dinner, because he was once a believer,
now a mocker of belief, because the sound
of his voice makes him happy and sad at once,
and he likes this feeling of mixing things.

When you go to sleep you hear the cat climb
up the stairs, you hear the ash remains
of the cousin groaning in your closet where jeans
that no longer fit you rest resentful for your wild
aging body. You hear him moan and groan
and cannot tell whether it is pleasure or pain.

And you savor such midnight thoughts,
which is why you, the cousin and the cat
are one in spontaneous revolt against time.
And Freud is there too, happy as a hotel clerk,
so you know it must be nothing but a dream.

# Searching for People

My grandmother is walking up the stairs
from the bathroom on the first floor
with its green tiles and mold,
its clogged drain and old pink bar of soap.

I squeeze my eyes closed and listen
to the rhythm of her feet on the stairs,
counting them like they are scales—
"every good boy does fine," like my piano teacher

reminds me every week. She's walking
up to her room next to mine.
Her cot squeaks a familiar squeak,
its music high-pitched and anxious.

She has already had her nightly dream.
And I've already waited for it,
waited for the digital clock to flip its numbers
to 12:34, numbers ordered as soldiers marching

to war. That's when she tosses
and turns, the antique clocks chime,
and Mommy and Daddy, on the same floor
inside the same house, sleep and snore

through all this night music. Omama wet
with sweat, me playing nurse with a washcloth
dampened in the sink. I don't know why
she wakes at night screaming words in German

I understand. These words are knives
in my throat. Terror words: *schnell schnell
zie kommen,* they're coming, and I tell her,
miming my mother's voice,

no one's coming, you are home, breathe,
have some water, Oma. By morning
she is composed, sipping black coffee
from a water glass with no handle.

She will sit on the couch,
keeping time as I play my scales,
then Mozart, then a sonata, then *Pathetique,*
a living statue, waving her porcelain arm
in the air. She lost her parents
in Theresienstadt. I just had to say it.
Her brother Alex and his four children
all young, 4, 6, 8, and the baby Alexandra.

His pretty wife Bea, all murdered in Auschwitz.
She lost her husband, my Opa Leo,
after whom I'm named. If she were
here in this room she would stop,

reach for a sesame candy Mommy
kept in a crystal bowl on a glass table.
With few teeth remaining, she'd chew
like a camel I once saw in Israel chew,

a graceful quiet camel with doe-eyes.
Her blonde hair swept into a lemony
chignon atop her regal head of horror.
Are you ready to play, Leeza?

Ready to go slowly, say only what is
essential. Otherwise be quiet.
Do you trust time to arrive in your hands?
Inside me lives her body that survived

the terror, her beloved German inside
and refusing to break down.
Stockings, black coffee, *butterbrot,*
and vodka, refusing to let go and live.

She was not unbroken: she read
*The Magic Mountain,* the *Aufbau,*
looking for names (I saw her do it),
searching for people with her index finger.

*Vas suchst du,* what are
you looking for, Oma?
She looks up as though I am
a stranger on a train. Then:

*Lass mich in Ruhe, mein Kind.*
Play something *lustig* for me.
Be so kind. She died every day.
I saw it. She's dying right now

inside me. No kidding.

# So strange to be alive

with the baby rocker gathering
light and clothes in the corner
and my father's antique clock,
its entire being—heart, liver, intestines,
undomed to the light like
a cathedral without a body
exposed to all the elements,

and me, here, on a Saturday morning,
still lying in a regal king-sized bed,
my husband's walked our daughter
to her morning art class in mixed media,
so strange that any minute
she will burst into the room
like a kangaroo escaped from the zoo,

like a star fallen from the sky,
and plop upon the regal bed
with its blue sheets rumpled
from a fitful night of sleep
where all my ancestors
lined up and held timepieces
in their hands like offerings—

sundials and digital clocks,
a grandfather clock balanced
in my mother's palm, a gold pocket watch
in my father's hands, wooden wall clocks,
swiss cuckoo clocks, French clocks
with crystal pendulums, all my father's
ancient clock collection, the ones I sold,

they were handing time back to me
their heads bowed, not solemnly but
as though they would explode with laughter
any second, they were solemn clowns of light
and time, waiting for me to rouse from sleep,
trickster-ancestors prodding me to wake,
and then it is I who wake

cracking up with a lightness and lack of fear
I am on a narrow bridge looking down
crying with laughter at all of creation
I could not stop laughing at how strange it is
to be alive, here, living with such wonderful
human beings, one of whom we created
with our own bodies, laughing and laughing

at the miracle of dust rocking the rocker
where moments before I had nursed
the infant who will burst into the regal room
where the black tuxedo cat named Shai
sits before me following my gold pen
traverse the page even as it all disappears
into one of Hashem's seventy silent faces

so strange to be alive to
listen to the purr of a cat who
leaves his black fur between
the letters, whose green almond eyes
stare at me oh, curious beloved, how
can death deign to exist?

Here she is now,
coming up the stairs,
she smells of sky, of blue,
of birds, of light, of that
which has no name
but love crackling open
again and again and again,
singing its dusty song

# Praying Mantis

I thought it was a grasshopper or a sprig of something
that fell from the tree

hovering over the monkey bars and snaky slide
where the toddlers played

what is it what is it they asked, pulling us over
with their little hands

their capes flowing back in the September wind
could it be a praying mantis

one of the mothers popped a potato chip into her mouth
she looked like a child all greasy black hair stringing down,

another reapplied her lip gloss
in a way I thought sexy but would never say

the children ran through a soccer field
rolled in the grass

they held hands let go of hands
they danced with the wind and spun and spun.

I sat at a picnic table telling a mother
the latest way my husband disappointed me

she wondered what she'd make for dinner,
gathered her blonde hair into a ponytail.

Our children returned, drenched from
the water fountain where they had become

temporary fish shivering now
for the sun has begun to set,

the praying mantis, a pale green
balancing ballerina, delicate

as a beating heart, my daughter's toes
in the moonlight, the children's eyes

crazy planets so innocent
they could birth prayer inside their gaze.

# My Father's Time

I try to find my father's time
inside mine. It is difficult.

His time was Enchanted. A dream
time he conjured with his hands.

My father almost died *over there.*
Good people saved him.

A boat saved him. Feces on the side
of the boat, according to one eye-witness.

Raw onions saved him.
My father laughed a lot.

The clocks in our house
he gathered like lost children,

chime and sing and gong
and cuckoo at all hours.

You see, really he lives in
No-Time. When he was hungry,

he ate. Half a loaf of Italian bread
once on his way home from work!

*Mickeylein, you won't be hungry
for dinner,* Mommy said.

But he ate the mushroom
soup, the kohlrabi lightly salted.

He asked for more. For dessert.
*Noch vas?* he asked, his voice an innocent lilt.

For me, time imprisons.
Narrow and narrowing. I am searching

for my father's time, which suffused
our Sundays when we all gathered

at the endless table full of cakes
and Turkish coffee brewed

in the old pot
Mommy brought from Israel.

Time weighs down on me.
What time is it?

Death skipped a generation.
He, so light, me, so dark,

he lightness mixed with human dark,
me darkness mixed with daddy's light.

Eye loupe, springs, mechanism, balance.
Steady as a clock. Rose at 6. Shower

and a cup of coffee light and sweet.
Off to work. Home to wash hands,

lots of soap at the sink upstairs.
His elegant hands splashing

grace notes under the faucet.
Always the same, without boredom.

A man of routine. Where will he go
after I die? Will he become a photo

with no name in an album. Who is that?
A man who was almost murdered

at a time when 1.5 million infants
were murdered. Why do you write

about such dark things, Leeza,
have a piece of chocolate,

bake a cake, be easy and light.
Listen to some Louis Armstrong.

Listen to such a beautiful sound he can
create from blowing into his trumpet.

Daddy closes his light brown eyes
and listens to the sound

Louis makes with his trumpet,
and time enraptured sways

over his head. Inside me
time is ticking-tocking

I am going to die
away from where I come from.

There is, yes, his time
inside of mine.

But it is difficult.

# Traversed

They traverse the same countries
my ancestors traversed.
The names remain inside me,

Moldavia, Slovenia, Slovakia,
like a broken lullaby
from my mother's lips.

Here, I want to say to the newborn refugees,
is an old map folded, creased, stained, and worn,
like a sheet that has sat in a closet for years,

pressed with time and moth balls.
This is how he made his way, his
Houdini-escape when he was forced out,

crossing borders and countries looking
for shelter. The forests knew him well.
Separated his cries of fear from his cries of pain.

Here, dear stranger, I want to say,
is a map of his route. It is old, some
of the names have changed, but the land

remains the same. The map is
not the territory, it's an old game.
Everything is and is not the same.

Here is some ink from his pen
where he marked a fork. Here is a spot
of something else. Dirt? No, blood.

He made it up to there and then nothing.
No one ever heard from him again.
His pregnant wife cried and cried.

One day, this map arrives, falls from
the sky, finds its way back somehow.
Who knows how things unfold for people.

I hope you arrive someplace safe.
I hope we hear from you again
so you can tell us where you have been.

After the skies settle, the cries
clear, the smoke dissolves,
and the rubble is removed.

My Zayde's name was Max, like mine.
This is the open grave
of my heart unfolded in time.

Tread lightly, fellow traveler.
He too was a refugee.
I hope you will find a home.

In the meantime,
there will be bread and stars,
and your old bed in the old room.

Your granddaughter remembers it,
will conjure it. She will reassemble you.
And what of the parts she makes up?

The most true, the most true.

# Poem in the Shape of an Enso

For a long time
after they died
there was an
emptiness, but

no circle around me
my self and Self were
not in rhythm with the ocean,
and on the beach of the ten thousand days
on the bay beside my childhood house—
no wildflower-infinity in
my grain of sight

I cried and cried
I attracted pits and debris
blowing in the wind inside me

I wish I could tell you
what changed
and how it changed
(even if I could,
still something
would be missing)

I wish I could say
I do not sit
waiting for the next
disaster. I wish
I could tell you
I trust life to
serve its raw realities
unbloodied and tender

What happened?
I stumbled
upon some luck: a man,
a daughter, two cats, a dog

I stumbled upon a house, a bed,
a lamp, spontaneous laughter

I bow into the memories
of my dead
when I receive
the mail from Tom
when I stir milk
into my coffee
when I gather
our girl off the yellow
bus, when I listen
to you shovel snow

I resolve to scribble
about my unresolve
until the gap
between my self
and my Self
is so small

a dinosaur's face
a dictator's face
a deer's face
is my own face
and nothing myself

I will behold the emptiness
that is not there
and the emptiness that is

(and then I will be with them
and you will be with me
with them here inside and out
the great circle)

# Human Race

*There is no art for art's sake. There are no, and cannot be "free"*
*artists, writers, poets, dramatists, directors or journalists, standing*
*above the society. Nobody needs them.*
                    —Uncle Joe Stalin, patron of the Jewish Arts

You cannot control what you will remember.
Today it snows and the snow collects
on the branches. In a room facing the street
two girls play, their sentences and laughter

mix with the sound of our neighbor
shoveling who is my father shoveling
snow on our driveway and me looking
out the window of my room above

the garage at my father's dancing body
making the shovel look light when it is heavy.
The scent of fried onions and boiled potatoes
rises up the stairs. My mother stands

at the kitchen counter squeezing
a lemon over salad greens
the space between her teeth suddenly larger
than yesterday, and sometimes she'll say

*I will call the dentist to see how much it would cost*
*to fix the space* which always surprises me
because there is nothing about her
that I think needs to be fixed.

Just as my daughter says *do not color*
*the grey with red because you are beautiful,*
*Mommy, no older than 35 plus, right?* She
winks at me and this wink is sublime,

the Meru of my world. As the lentil soup
simmers I read Brodsky's Nobel speech,
something has led me to him today. I read too
how Lenin denounced his poetry as *pornographic*

and *anti-Soviet* and sent him to a mental institute.
He was charged with *social parasitism* in his 1964 trial.
Today I open my eyes at 7:14, our black tuxedo
cat named Shai, which means *gift* in Hebrew,

is coiled up beside my body, his sleepy
bedroom eyes already full of the impending snow.
I bury my face in his fur and inhale deeply.
My feet touch the cold bathroom tiles. I pee

and brush my teeth. Today I baked gluten-free
brownies with two little girls who stirred and licked
the bowl the way I did when my mother and I
baked almond crescent cookies. I see her

strong hands rolling the dough into little moons
and dusting the hot crescents with confectioner's sugar.
Today I graded papers, made dinner, lit the Hanukkah candles,
watched my husband shovel snow, hoping he would not get a

heart attack and saying so: *Be careful not to get*
*a heart attack*, I say, as he slips the one leather glove
that remains from last year's gift onto his right hand.
*And what about your other hand?* I ask him as he

opens the door. Either he did not respond or I do
not remember or it was the wind or the snow or
the girls playing with the Barbie Adventure House.
And later while my daughter dreams upstairs,

I work as a poet downstairs, and thankfully, no one,
not even my lost parents, cares. My father
steps aboard a boat named the Noemi Julia.
He is 19, a boy from Berlin who loves to tinker

with clocks and radios. In 1939 he steps on a boat
that will take him to Palestine with onions on his breath.
I think of my father as I chop onions. The girls are hungry
and stand waiting for hot brownies. My eyes tear. *Why*

*are you crying, Mommy? Are you sad that the snow*
*will turn to ice? Are you sad Alexandra cannot stay*
*for dinner?* The girls sit at the table, their feet do not
touch the floor. Chocolate at the corner of their pink mouths.

They lick their fingers. *No thank you, yes please,*
*I don't care for milk.* We live for each other
or not at all. My mother died before she
fixed her teeth. I buried her as Jews do

in a plain pine box. I kiss her cold face. I say words
in Hebrew I don't fully understand that have to do
with God, mercy, memory and peace. Since they
lowered the lid I have never been the same.

I do the dishes after my daughter sleeps.
Outside red and white Christmas lights
blink on and off. Snow covers the city
streets. My dead are never far from me.

Joe, this is my art for art's sake—
a woman's tears, chopping onions,
remembering for the future of girls
and their polite dangling feet.

On an average winter day
with the omniscient missing God.

# About the Author

Pushcart nominee and Temple University English Professor Lisa Grunberger is a first-generation American writer. Her award winning poetry book *I am dirty* (Moonstone Press) and *Born Knowing* (Finishing Line Press) are lyrical reflections on life as a woman, a mother, and a daughter of Holocaust survivors. Her book *Yiddish Yoga: Ruthie's Adventures in Love, Loss and the Lotus Position* (HarperCollins) is currently being adapted as a musical.

She is a widely published poet whose work has appeared in *The New York Times, The Paterson Literary Review, Mudfish, The Drunken Boat, Bridges: A Jewish Feminist Journal, Philadelphia Stories, Paroles des Jour, Dialogi, Crab Orchard Review, Mom Egg Review, The Baffler,* and *Fine Linen Press.* Her story about motherhood, adoption and infertility, "Inheritance" appears in the anthology *Infertilities: A Curation* (Wayne State University Press). Whether it is the aging woman's body, the infertile body, the body ravaged by war and trauma, all her work addresses human embodiment in a philosophical, spiritual, tender and satirical  voice. Her poems have been translated into Hebrew, Slovenian, Russian, Spanish, and Yiddish. *Almost Pregnant,* her play about infertility and assisted reproductive technologies, is published by Next Stage Press. Her play *Alexa Talks to Rebecca* won the Audience Choice Award at the Squeaky Bicycle Theatre. Lisa teaches Yoga and Writing workshops and lives with her family in Philadelphia. She is working on a memoir called *Me and My Makers: An Adopted Woman's Double Holocaust Inheritance.*

Her website is:
www.Lisa-Grunberger.com

Printed in the USA
CPSIA information can be obtained
at www.ICGtesting.com
LVHW021800070324
773837LV00001B/124